How To Do a
Science Project

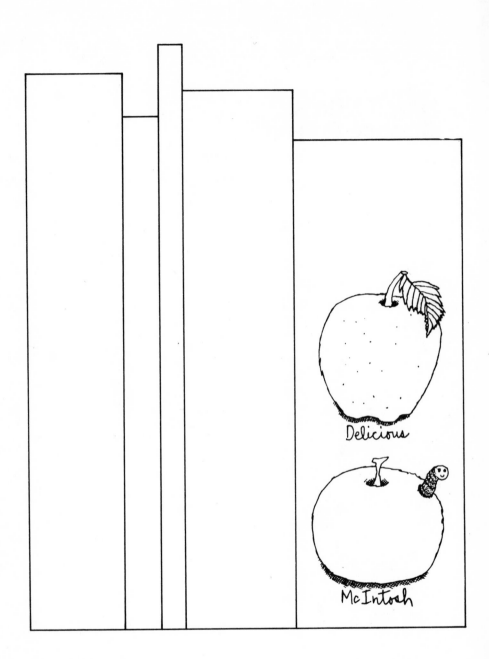

Delicious

McIntosh

HOW TO DO A
SCIENCE PROJECT

BY DAVID WEBSTER

**ILLUSTRATED WITH
PHOTOGRAPHS
AND DRAWINGS**

FRANKLIN WATTS | NEW YORK | LONDON
◄─A FIRST BOOK─►

Illustrations on pages 6 and 34 copyright © 1960 by Stanley and Janice Berenstain.

All other illustrations were redrawn by Carolyn Bentley from material prepared by students for science project presentations. The students who contributed writing and artwork for this volume are listed in the Acknowledgments on page 57.

The photographs on pages 8 and 49 courtesy of the Lincoln Public Schools of Lincoln, Massachusetts. All other photographs were taken by the author.

Library of Congress Cataloging in Publication Data

Webster, David, 1930-
    How to do a science project.

    (A First book)
    Bibliography: p.
    SUMMARY: Suggestions for three types of science projects—report, demonstration, and research—with emphasis on procedures used to do a successful research project.
    1. Science — Experiments — Juvenile literature.
[1. Science — Experiments] I. Title.
Q163.W38   502'.8   73-12214
ISBN 0-531-00817-7

Contents

How To Do a
Science Project

Introduction

Science and experimenting go hand in hand. Scientists solve problems by making observations and by conducting experiments. Such activities are known as science research. By doing a science project, you should learn how scientists work to solve problems.

When doing a science project, you must first decide upon a suitable topic for investigation. Then you write a plan that tells how you expect to proceed. As your project is carried out, you will observe, experiment, and draw conclusions based on your results. In the end, you will write a detailed report to inform others of your research. You might also present an oral report or construct a project display for a science fair.

Like most worthwhile schoolwork, a science project is not an easy job. It will require a lot of time, thought, and just plain work. But you will receive plenty of satisfaction from a well-done project. There is no better way to understand what real science is all about.

Selecting
a Problem

Perhaps the hardest part of doing a science project is getting an idea to work on. If you find a good topic, you should be able to develop a good science project. An unsuitable topic can rarely be turned into a good project no matter how much work you do.

You might be able to use a science interest that you already have. Do you like turtles, or rocks, or motors? Perhaps you have done some experimenting with a microscope, a chemistry kit, or model rockets.

If you don't have a strong interest in anything scientific, there are several other ways for you to get project ideas. Ask your teacher for suggestions. The teacher may have a list of projects that were done by students in past years. Maybe your parents would be able to offer good advice, too. Your library probably has a few books that would help you to select an interesting project. On page 51 there is a list of books that should be useful.

Safety should be kept in mind when you pick a project. You should not plan to use poisons, explosives, high voltage, or harmful bacteria. Experiments on animals are alright as long as the animal is not injured. You cannot dissect, starve, or mistreat any live animal.

There are three different types of science projects: a report project, a demonstration project, and a research project. A report project is merely a written report based on what you have learned by reading. A demonstration project, however, includes real materials or devices. The best kind of project is the research project, because it is a true scientific investigation.

☐ Report Projects

This is the easiest type of project since it requires only reading and writing. It is really no different from other kinds of school reports on books about history or art or music. A report project is not usually as much fun as a demonstration project or a research project.

Here is a list of some report projects that students have done:

Electricity	Dinosaurs	Whales
Light bulbs	Plants	Tooth decay
Matches	Ants	Bacteria
Atoms	Geology	Rockets
Fish	Eyes	Molds
Volcanoes	Clocks	Erosion
Glass	Fingerprinting	Transistors
Porcupines	Teeth	Outer space
Photography	Earth	Crystals
Oxygen	Caves	Clouds

"Perhaps we'd have been better off with the caterpillars"

Most of these sound pretty dull, don't they? What you probably like most about science are the things you *do*, such as collecting rocks, building an electrical gadget, or making a salt water aquarium. These activities lead to demonstration projects.

☐ **Demonstration Projects**

There are many kinds of good demonstration projects. You could make a collection, perform an experiment, or construct a scientific device. The important thing is for you to do something instead of just reading and writing.

Perhaps you already have begun a collection of seashells or bird nests. For a project you could try to add more shells or nests to the collection. Of course, you should also read about what you are collecting in books from the library. Here are some things you could collect:

Minerals	Bones
Weed seeds	Seashells
Local soils	Skulls
Bird nests	Preserved snowflakes
Track casts	Tree buds
Homemade crystals	Spider webs

Do you like to make gadgets with wood, wire, and tin cans? Why not build something for a project? If you cannot find plans for what you want to construct, invent your own design.

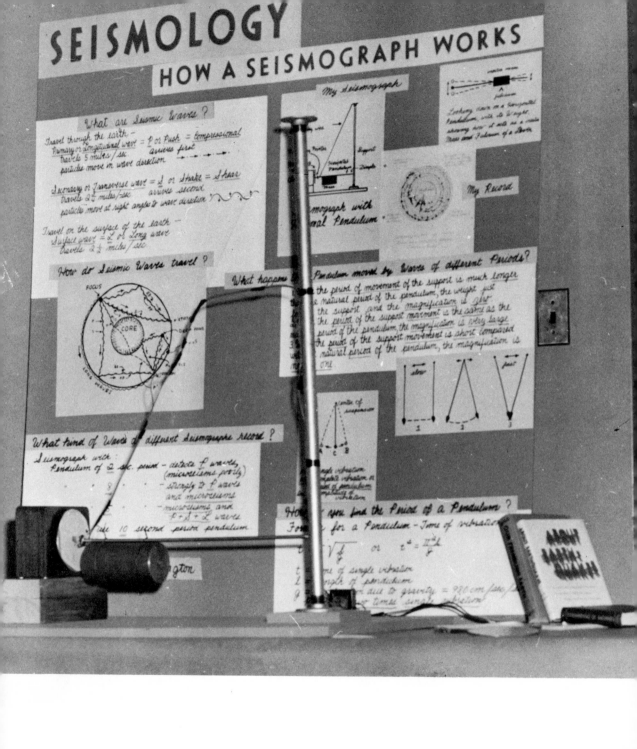

Below is a list of gadgets that science students have created:

Incubator for hatching eggs
Electronic computer
Reflector telescope
Reaction timer
Ripple tank
Strobe light
Crystal diode radio
Model steam engine
Homemade seismograph
Lie detector
Homemade camera
Arc lamp
Ballistic pendulum
Telegraph set
Sand pendulum
Wind tunnel
Burglar alarm
Homemade thermometer
Trash Can Harry (junk robot)

Almost everyone likes to experiment. Demonstration experiments are usually pretty good projects. You have probably done experiments during your science classes in school. Maybe you would enjoy doing one of these:

A project on how
a seismograph works.

Copper plating
Gerbils in a maze
Purifying water
Hatching brine shrimp
Growth of bacteria
Expansion of metals
Reaction of protozoa
Measuring earth's circumference
How sound is produced
Developing film
Chemical experiments
Nutrition of rats
Paper chromatography
Force of freezing water
Electrolysis of water
Changing salt water to fresh water
Rate of acceleration
Chick hatching
Measuring distance to moon
Photosynthesis demonstration

☐ **Research Projects**

The best kind of project is a research project. Research is what real science is all about. The title of a research project is usually in the form of a question. But you don't know the answer to the question before you begin. Your experiments and observations help you to answer the question yourself. In some projects you still may not know the answer when the project has been completed.

You are not expected to do original research — something that has never been done before. The answer to almost any question is known by at least some scientists.

Do not think that your question needs to be a difficult one; usually a simple question makes the best project. It would be foolish for you to try to solve such questions as "What chemicals are in a tomato?" or "How does a dog learn to bark?" It is much better to do a good job on a little question than a poor job on a big question.

One suitable area for research is the testing of advertising claims made for certain products. Many TV commercials should suggest projects to you.

What is the strength of different paper towels?
What brand of bread stays fresh longest?
What building material is the best insulator?
What dog food does my dog like best?
Which detergent cleans best?
Do toothpastes really kill mouth bacteria?

You might be interested in developing a special technique for measuring something very small or extremely thin.

How much does a fly weigh?
Can the thickness of a soap bubble be measured?
How can the size of paramecia be measured?
How many scales does a butterfly have on its wings?
How can the water content of foods be computed?
How can the hardness of different woods be tested?

One of the most common kinds of research project

involves making changes in a physical system. Everyone knows that water in a glass slowly evaporates. What can you do to make the water evaporate faster? How much heat is necessary to cause the evaporation rate to double? Would water dyed red evaporate more quickly? To answer these questions or the ones below, the experimenter must change conditions and observe what effects occur.

How does temperature affect crystal growth rate?

What shape glass causes water to cool off fastest?

Do weight and surface tension affect drop size?

How does the size of a balloon affect its pressure?

What conditions favor the rusting of iron?

How does a balloon's diameter influence its rate of descent?

How does salt concentration affect the freezing temperature of water?

How can the strength of an electromagnet be increased?

Animals and plants can also be studied for a research project.

How does the weather affect birds' eating habits?

Can goldfish live in salt water?

How do light and temperature affect bread mold growth?

Will artificial colors alter a cat's food preference?

How is human reaction time changed under different conditions?

How is the growth of bean plants affected by different fertilizers?

The "Scientific Method"

Some people think scientists have a special way to solve problems. This technique of research is often called the *scientific method*. But scientists themselves know that there is no certain way to conduct investigations. Each problem has special conditions that require different procedures.

There are, however, some basic principles that guide most scientific effort. The most important of these are listed below:

1. Reference to authority
2. Observation
3. Trial and error
4. Experimental control
5. The need for repetition
6. Sources of error

If you have some understanding of these principles, you should be able to do a better research project.

☐ Reference to Authority

Before a scientist does anything, he usually spends a lot of time reading. He attempts to find out what other work has already been done that relates to his problem.

Reports of research conducted all over the world are published in a variety of scientific journals. You might be able to find some information on your project in a library book. Ask the librarian for help.

☐ Observation

You observe with your senses of sight, hearing, touch, taste, and smell. Scientists have developed special substances and tools that allow them to extend their senses. For example, the presence of starch is detected by the purple color that results when iodine is added. Minute bacteria can be seen only through a high-powered microscope.

Scientists must be keen observers. Naturalists who study animal behavior spend countless hours watching wild creatures. Perhaps you have heard of Jane Goodall who lived in Africa for two years in order to observe baboons. Astronomers, too, have made great discoveries about the universe by looking at stars through gigantic telescopes. You will need to observe carefully even if your project deals only with a rolling ball or pieces of string.

☐ Trial and error

Often scientists solve problems by making different tests and then noticing what happens. If your father's car does not start some morning, he might use the same trial and error procedure to find out what is wrong with it. First he might check to see if there is gasoline in the tank. Then he would probably see if the wires were wet or if the spark plugs were sparking. Of course, your father must know something about how the car engine runs so he can make the right tests. It would be foolish to check the air in the tires or to see if the back windows were up.

☐ Experimental control

Suppose a scientist wants to find out why potatoes grow better in Maine than they do in Florida. His guess is that the weather is too warm in Florida for growing potatoes. To prove this, he plants potatoes in Florida inside a large box that can be kept cool. But the potato plants still do not grow well, so the careless scientist concludes that temperature is not important. What he has forgotten is that there are other differences between Florida and Maine that might explain plant growth variation. Among these variables are soil structure, rainfall, day length, and even latitude. To answer the question, experiments must be designed to test these variables one at a time.

☐ The need for repetition

In most experiments it is not enough to do something just once. A student experimenting with ice found that an ice cube took 53 minutes to melt in a glass of water. The boy's teacher suggested that he try the experiment several more times. In the next tests, the ice cube melted in 46 minutes and in 51 minutes. Averaging the three numbers gave a more accurate time of 50 minutes.

□ Sources of error

Why did the ice cube melt in different times? No matter how hard you try, it is never possible to keep all conditions the same. Ice cubes are not all exactly the same size and shape. Ice melting time would also be affected by the amount and temperature of the water in the glass. Perhaps the student made mistakes in measuring the time the ice cube took to melt. Maybe he forgot to label the glasses and they got mixed up. When you perform experiments, you must be continually aware of errors that will influence your results. Try to eliminate as many errors as possible before you begin.

Some problems with my
chemical tests on suntan lotion [1]

According to trial one, Coppertone Suntan Lotion, Coppertone Noskote, and Presun Lotion were the best in absorbing ultraviolet rays. There is a problem in trial one, though, because it had nothing to absorb the rays. So I knew I did something wrong. I did the experiment over and this time I did not put the sunlamp so close to the tubes. Also, I weighed each piece of filter paper separately, because for trial 1 I just weighed one and figured all the rest weighed the same.

Preliminary Work

Before you actually begin to experiment or build equipment, you should do some planning. Find out as much as you can about your subject from people and books. Then write a plan telling what you expect to do.

You might be able to find an adult who can offer you good advice. If you live near a university, you could ask a professor in the science department. Most museums have an educational staff who could give you help. Perhaps there is someone living near you who could give you good ideas.

While it is alright to get help from someone, you must not allow others to do too much. The project is your own. Sometimes an adult becomes so excited by your work that he begins to "take over." Tell him politely that you would rather do the project yourself.

You should certainly look for information in your school or town library. All libraries have a thick volume called *Subject Guide to Books in Print.* This book contains a list of all books that are currently available, listed under subject headings. Thus if your project were related to insulation, you could check the listings under "insulation," "building materials," and "heat." Another reference book called *Readers' Guide to Periodical Literature* gives information on magazine articles. However, keep in mind that you may not be able to find any written material that relates to your project — especially if your subject is a highly original one.

☐ **The logbook**

Before you read any books or magazines, you should get a "logbook." The project log is merely a booklet of blank pages bound together. You use the log as sort of a science diary to record everything about your project. The logbook can have lined or blank pages, whichever you prefer. Since separate sheets of paper can get lost, loose-leaf notebooks are not usually used.

The first entries in your log will probably be notes taken as you read. You don't have to write too much, or even use complete sentences. Just put down enough to remember the main points you have read. Also, be sure to note what book the information came from, in case you want to recheck something later.

☐ **The project plan**

A plan should be written to outline how you expect to carry out your project. Of course, you will never follow the plan exactly. As your work progresses, you will find that some of your initial plans are not practical. And new ideas will develop that you had not thought of before. But, even though it is imperfect, the plan provides a starting point so you can at least begin.

Your plan should contain four main parts:

1. A statement of the problem
2. A description of what you are going to do
3. A list of needed materials
4. A time schedule

☐ The problem statement

The title of a research project is usually best expressed as a question. Which of the following statements do you think gives the clearest explanation of what the project is about:

1. Growing yeast
2. Yeast growth and temperature
3. How does temperature affect the growth of yeast?

Sometimes it is possible to write a brief statement that is just as good as a question. For example, the yeast project could be titled, "The Effect of Temperature on Yeast Growth."

In writing your title, you should avoid making it too long. If you try to tell too much in your question, it can become unclear. Which of the two questions below would you prefer for a project title:

1. Is an animal's respiration rate related to its size?
2. What are the respiration rates of a mouse, a rabbit, a cat, a dog, a pony, and a cow, and are the rates related to the animals' sizes, or to some other factors such as the animal's age, its previous activity, its diet, the time of day, or the air temperature?

☐ What are you going to do

The main part of your plan should be a complete description of what you expect to do. Drawings should be used to show how you will construct homemade equipment or arrange experimental apparatus.

☐ Materials needed

It is important to plan for the materials you will need in your investigation. Sometimes a project becomes impossible when necessary equipment is not available. In listing your materials, include the source and cost of each item required.

Of course, the most convenient place to find things is around your home. Be sure to ask your parents before you take anything from the kitchen, medicine cabinet, or cellar shelves. A great variety of supplies can be purchased from stores that sell food, drugs, and hardware. Specialized equipment is more difficult to obtain. You might be able to borrow some laboratory equipment from the high school science teacher.

☐ Time schedule

Like most people, you probably put off doing jobs until the last minute. Many a good project has failed when the experimenter ran out of time. A schedule will help you to get your project completed on time.

You should estimate how many weeks it will take for

you to accomplish each part of your project. Then schedule each step, counting back from the date your project is due. Since things almost always take longer than you expect, allow plenty of extra time.

Sample Student Plan(2)

Problem Statement: Which way will a gerbil go, to food or freedom?

What I am going to do: First I am going to build a simple T maze with chicken wire over the top so I can see in. Then I am going to put a gerbil in the maze with food at one end of the crossbar and an open door to freedom at the other end. I will also try other experiments, such as: which way will it go with both sides of the crossbar closed, or which way will it go with both ends open?

Materials List: One or two gerbils — Mr. W.
Aquarium — Mr. W.
Half-inch square chicken wire —
  Mr. W.?
Wood shavings — school
Gerbil food — home or school

Time Schedule: Feb. 1-7: Get materials
Feb. 7-14: Build maze
Feb. 14-21: Do experiments
Feb. 21-Mar. 2: Write report

Doing
the
Research

It is important to have a definite work area for your experiments. At home, it could be in your room if there is no danger of spilling on the floor. Messy projects should be done in the cellar or garage. Protect your equipment from being damaged by pesky pets and curious babies. Your project might be done at school if your teacher approves.

Your investigations will probably require many weeks. During this time you should make daily entries in your logbook. Write a complete account of all that you do. Sometimes, what seems unimportant when you do it proves to be of much value later. You will forget a lot of useful information unless everything is written down.

The logbook should look somewhat like a diary, with the pages divided into separate days. You need not use complete sentences. You can even write sloppily, as long as you can read it. The information from the logbook is used when your final report is prepared.

Perhaps the first thing you will find out after you begin is that things don't happen as you expect. Your seeds don't sprout or your bottles break or your little sister dumps out all the chemicals. Try not to become discouraged and give up. With a little more work you can make corrections so things go better next time.

Description of experiment
on inertia measurement (3)

I was thinking of using a skateboard and bringing it to a line several inches from a wall and propelling it into the wall. At first I thought of springs then a ramp but elastics seemed the best. I took a piece of wood the size of a ruler and put the elastic on the end pulling it like an arrow. I put the other end on the skateboard and let it go. I took a piece of cardboard about 18″ by 5″ and put quarter inch marks on it to measure the distance and for a wider runway. I used this platform for the other experiment also. My materials were:
1. a piece of cardboard 18 by 5
2. a large rubber elastic
3. 2 wooden blocks
4. a 2½ inch piece of tape

May 5 All afternoon I disturbed the Kisembe Group whenever I got closer than 50 yards. We followed them but they are quite shy of the car. In moving closer to the baboons, I frightened them and they ran toward the dam. Crip ran for 50 yards and then stopped and walked 50 yards behind the rest, carrying his injured foot close to the body. Is it a coincidence that all the injured baboons I have seen are injured in the right front foot? If this continues to be true, it would give some reason for believing that baboons use the right hand more than the left. My impression to date is that they use both hands equally when they feed.

June 19, 1:10. The playing of juveniles goes through a sort of cycle. They come up to each other playfully — that is, with a bouncing walk and holding their hands up in front of them. Then they begin to reach for each other's shoulders. As soon as they are holding on to each other, they begin to touch each other's necks and shoulders with their mouths open and their teeth showing. This is something I've never seen adults do. Usually one will start to run away and the other will chase it, pulling at its tail. Often they are most active if they have a rock or a small bush or a whistling thorn tree to play on and then they go around and around in a circle. One will run up the tree, hang for a moment, and drop, and then another one above will be ready to drop. Then the first one runs up the tree and drops again, often dropping on top of the next one's head.

☐ Results

As your work progresses, you should begin to get results. In experiments involving plants and animals, your results are often in the form of observations. You might notice that some plants have turned yellow or that your gerbil begins to chew up the plastic tube instead of the wooden block. Such observations are known as *qualitative* results since precise numbers are not involved. Animal behavior experiments often yield extensive notes describing the reactions of the animal being studied.

On the opposite page is a brief selection of field notes made by Professor DeVore as he studied baboon behavior in Kenya, Africa.

In physical science investigation, the results usually include numbers. When you make measurements of distance, weight, and time, you obtain *quantitative* results. Such numbers are often referred to as experimental data.

Data can be recorded most conveniently on a table. To make a table, you must first decide what information you expect to record. If you were measuring the freezing rate of water, for example, your table would have spaces for time and for the water's temperature. The table in the logbook does not have to be especially neat with straight lines drawn with a ruler. You will make finished tables to accompany your final report. The examples on the following pages may give you some ideas.

OVER-ALL LOOK AT STRENGTH AND ABSORPTION OF PAPER TOWELS

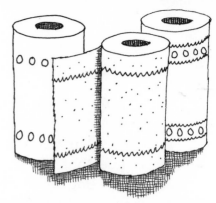

NAME	AMOUNT OF STRENGTH		AMOUNT OF ABSORPTION	
	1ST.	2ND.	1ST. (out of 4 oz.)	2ND. (out of 6 oz.)
A&P	didn't hold up	* ½-1 pound	2¾ oz. of water	3⅓ oz. of water
BOUNTY	1½ pounds	½-1½ pounds	3 oz. of water	4 oz. of water
SCOTT	1 pound	½-1 pound	2¼ oz. of water	3 oz. of water
VIVA	1½ pounds	½-1½ pounds	4 oz. of water	4½ oz. of water

* this shows how A&P made a remarkable comeback

FINAL RESULTS OF EATING PREFERENCES OF GERBILS and MICE

	ate the whole thing		ate more than half		ate some, but less than half		didn't eat any		
	Max	Neeper	Max	Neeper	Max	Neeper	Max	Neeper	
Sunflower seeds	✳	✳							SAME OPINIONS ON FOOD
Rabbit pellets					✳	✳			
Carrot peels							✳	✳	
Apple pulp			✳	✳					
Apple peels							✳	✳	
Water	✳	✳							
Lettuce	✳	✳							
Raw Hamburger	✳	✳							
Carrot pulp				✳		✳	✳		DIFFERENT OPINIONS ON FOOD
Pretzels		✳					✳		
chocolate chip cookies				✳			✳		
Stoned wheat thins	✳							✳	
Premium crackers			✳					✳	
velveta cheese		✳	✳						
cream cheese		✳					✳		

Max: Gerbil   Neeper: Mouse

(6)

The interesting thing I noticed was right
when the flame went out. There was a
cloud of smoke going up and once it
hit the top of the aquarium, smoke droplets
started coming down and then breaking up
into smaller ones until there was
nothing left.

☐ Illustrations

Another way to record results is with drawings. Make rough sketches in your logbook with pencil, and use labels to explain parts that cannot be drawn clearly. Most scientists are not good artists, so don't worry if your drawings look funny.

Photographs can also be used to illustrate your research. For indoor experiments you should have a flash attachment for the camera. Color film is not necessary. Paste small photos in your logbook on the appropriate pages. If your camera uses film that makes negatives, you can have some larger photographs made later to go with your report.

☐ Conclusions

When your experiments have been completed, you should be able to reach some conclusions. You still might be unable to answer your original question, however. Don't be afraid to say that you were unsuccessful in completely solving your problem. In the course of conducting your research, you certainly learned a great deal about the methods of science.

During your experiment you should be alert for other questions that arise. Make notes of these and provide answers later if you can. Much of what you learn from your project may be in areas that were unknown to you in the beginning.

Logbook photos —
Above: Materials for
a suntan lotion experiment.
Opposite: sunlamp shining
on test tubes for
a suntan lotion experiment.

*Some conclusions from research
on meat tenderizer* (7).

The results were hard to figure out because instead of getting softer the lamb and the beef got
tougher. Only the veal got softer which is what I
don't understand. I think that since hardly anyone
eats raw meat, you don't really know how soft the
meat is before it's cooked and then you sprinkle
the meat with tenderizer and cook it. Then when
you eat it you think it has softened the meat but in
my experiment I found out it doesn't really.

☐ **Experiment errors**

In writing your conclusions you should include com-
ments on any errors that could have affected your work.
No matter how hard you try, you cannot make perfect
measurements. You might have a watch that runs a little
slow or a ruler that is a tiny bit too long. Even more measurement errors are caused by mistakes made by the per-
son doing the measuring. You have a better chance of
avoiding the error if you repeat the measurement quite a
few times and figure an average.

Many experiments involve finding out how certain factors influence a reaction. For example, one student wanted
to find out which type of soil produced the best growth of

corn seedlings. He was surprised when the plants grew better in the sandy subsoil than they did in the rich topsoil. His teacher wondered if the topsoil had become so wet that the seedlings got rotten and moldy. Since more of the water evaporated from the sandy soil, the seeds grew better. The student wanted to test different types of soil. But without knowing it, he was really testing the water content of the soil. He had not *controlled the variables.* How should this experiment be done correctly?

It is extremely difficult to control all variables in experiments on animal behavior. Animals react to a great many stimuli. It is the experimenter's task to design an experiment that will test only the variables he wants. However, it is never possible to do this completely.

Be sure to admit that the truth of your conclusions is limited. Explain what errors of measurement and uncontrolled variables could have influenced your results. Are there other types of errors possible in your experiment?

Limitations in experiment with meat tenderizer [8]

Some of the errors I made were when I was holding the container on the meat I think I pushed the pins in a little bit by accident so the number of marbles it took might be wrong. Also I think I made a few mistakes counting the marbles.

In all your reporting you should be honest. You might be tempted to cheat if your results do not come out as you thought they would. One often hears the excuse, "The experiment didn't work." But if you think about it, an experiment always "works." When you say that an experiment doesn't work, you mean that it did not turn out in the way you expected. There have even been cases in which real scientists altered the results of their research to fit their own expectations. Be sure to report what really happened, and not what you hoped would happen.

The
Written
Report

A complete report of your project should be written when your research has been finished. You should prepare a written report even if you plan to make an oral report or a project display later. The paper must be written in enough detail so that the reader could repeat your research if he wanted. Many scientists are poor writers, but this should not be an excuse for sloppy writing. Your project can be improved with a polished write-up; a poor report can ruin even the most successful research.

The project report is written in the same manner as any other paper. First make a rough draft that can be checked by your teacher. Leave plenty of space between lines to allow room for corrections. Don't worry too much about spelling and punctuation on the rough draft. Think about what you want to say and express it clearly.

A good report will probably include the following parts:

1. Acknowledgments —
   An expression of thanks to people who helped
2. Discussion of problem —
   An explanation of the question
   and your reasons for selecting it
3. Materials and methods —
   What you did
4. Observations and results —
   What you found out
5. Conclusions —
   The answers to your original question
6. Limitations —
   Experiment errors
7. Bibliography —
   List of any books you read

If you have kept a complete logbook, it will contain all the information needed for the report. But you should not merely recopy whole sections from your log. In some places it will be necessary to reorganize the logbook notes. In other parts you may want to summarize information or to eliminate certain sections altogether.

When the first copy is completed, read it over carefully and correct all spelling and grammar errors. Let your teacher read it after you have made the corrections. Your final report should have good paragraphs and complete sentences. It should be neatly written in ink on white lined paper. Keep the left-hand margin straight.

(9)

Stick is placed on back end of skateboard. Elastic is drawn back like a bow and arrow. Stick is released and skateboard is propelled into wall.

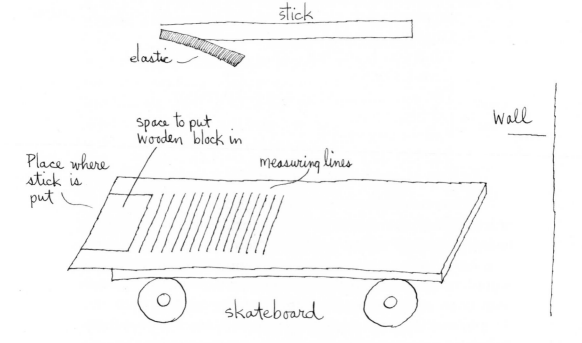

stick

elastic

space to put
wooden block in

measuring lines

Place where
stick is
put

Wall

skateboard

INERTIA EXPERIMENT

☐ Drawings

A final report should be illustrated with photographs or drawings. A scientific drawing is always done in pencil on plain white paper. Never use ink or colored pencils. Make the drawing large enough to fit the paper's size. If you are unable to draw well, try to find someone who is a better artist to make your drawings. Mention the artist's name in the acknowledgments.

The drawing should have a title printed beneath it. A scale should be used if it is necessary to show size. All labels should be printed, and the lines to them should not cross one another. Also, do not end the lines with arrows.

☐ Graphs

Often the best way to present your data is with a graph. When the numbers from a table are shown by a line, their significance is usually more apparent.

For graphs, use special graph paper that is ruled with eight lines per inch. When drawing the horizontal and vertical lines, leave enough space for the scales. Plan the divisions so there is enough space to mark all the necessary points. In some graphs the line need not pass through all the points. Draw a smooth curve that comes closest to the most points. The points often do not fall in a perfect line because of experimental errors.

(10) DEHYDRATION OF APPLES

Procedure: Taking two types of apples, McIntosh and Delicious, we sliced each in half and set them out at room temperature for a period of thirty-five days. We took weights periodically and made observations and conclusions from them. We graphed our results.

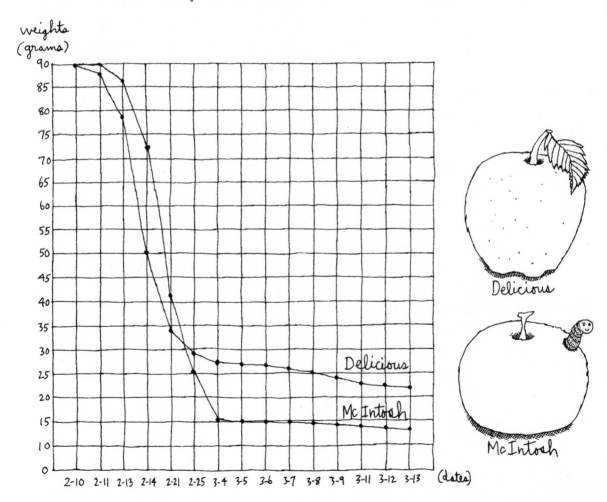

CANDLE BURNING TIME IN DIFFERENT SIZED JARS

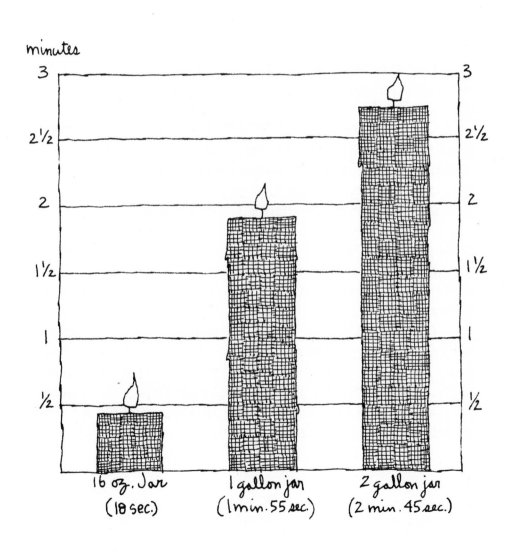

minutes

16 oz. Jar
(18 sec.)

1 gallon jar
(1 min. 55 sec.)

2 gallon jar
(2 min. 45 sec.)

The
Oral
Report

Your teacher may want you to give the class an oral report on your project. This will give you a chance to share what you learned with other young scientists.

The worst way to give an oral report would be to read a written report. What you should do is know the written report well enough so you can talk about it. Practice your talk, but don't memorize it. If you have a tape recorder, you can talk into it and then listen to yourself.

Many speakers like to make notes on their talk so they can remember the different points they want to cover. You can glance at your notes occasionally as you speak. The report should not be too long or your audience will become bored.

Your report will be more interesting if you have some materials or large posters to show. You could bring some of your equipment and leave it in the room for everyone to see. Large charts and pictures might be helpful to explain your results and conclusions. Plan how you will mount the visual aids so the audience can view them as you talk.

Remember, you know more about your project than anyone else in the room. Don't be afraid to speak loudly so everyone can hear you clearly. At the end of your talk, ask if there are any questions. If you have made an interesting presentation, some of the students will probably want to know more about your research. Take criticism gracefully, and, when necessary, say, "I don't know."

Student notes for talk (12)

My question is, "How much sugar and yeast are needed to make carbon dioxide?"

Tiny cells — carbon dioxide

Mostly grow in sugar

Ingredients — How to do it

Trapped air

Chart

Alcohol drink

Project
Display

Perhaps the most interesting way to explain your project is with a display. Often your display can be set up in your classroom. If other students are showing their projects at the same time, children from other classes might want to come in and look at them. Some schools have Science Fairs, where many projects are displayed in the gymnasium or other large room. Projects at a science fair are usually judged so prizes can be awarded to the best ones.

Your display should be designed so that it fits into the space that is available. You will probably need a table in front of a bulletin board for hanging papers. Large pieces of cardboard can be taped together to make a large background that will stand on the back of the table.

The first thing one should notice when looking at a display is the project's title. A good way to make a neat sign is to cut large letters out of colored paper. It is also possible to buy ready-made letters in some stationery stores. Under the title you should hang some large photographs or pictures. These drawings should be done in color to make them attractive. You could also make large charts and graphs to mount on the bulletin board.

Some of your equipment or specimens should be placed on the table. These are what most people are interested in. Live animals and moving mechanical devices are especially good for attracting attention. Avoid displaying anything that can be easily broken or that might injure someone. Valuable items should not be left out on display, since they might disappear when you are not looking. Your logbook and written report should be on the table.

You should stand with your project during the times that others are viewing it. Show spectators a little bit about what you have done. Don't bore people with a long speech. If someone is more interested, he will ask you questions.

In a science fair you will probably be quizzed by judges. Don't be afraid to speak up and talk to them. You will know more about your project than even most of the judges. Answer questions honestly, and always admit when you don't know something. It helps to make a good impression on the judges if you are dressed neatly.

You are to be congratulated if your project earns a prize. Your hard work has paid off. But even if you are not rewarded with a prize, your time has not been wasted. You have carried out a real research project and learned quite a bit about how scientists solve problems.

Over : Energy crisis project.

ANSWERS to the ENERGY

Hydrogen Fuel

Electricity from nuclear fuels

Electrolysis of water

ENERGY

Solar Energy

These work 5 level Solar Power collection Satelites, that would beam power back to earth.

In order for the above to work, hydrogen fuel would have to team up with atomic energy. The electricity from nuclear fuels would be used in the electrolysis of water. This process separtes the hydrogen and oxygen. The oxygen could be used to restore our polluted waters. The steel companys would be stored and transp would be stored and transp conduction areas. When thi of hydrogen takes place, the fuel element ever known to m release greatamounts of energy product is pure water, in fact you can drink it, as our ast The pure water goes into natu enviroment as rain. It wou a matter of days or weeks to r before. Much faster than foss take millions of years to re

SUN
Simulater

Solar Cells

Storage

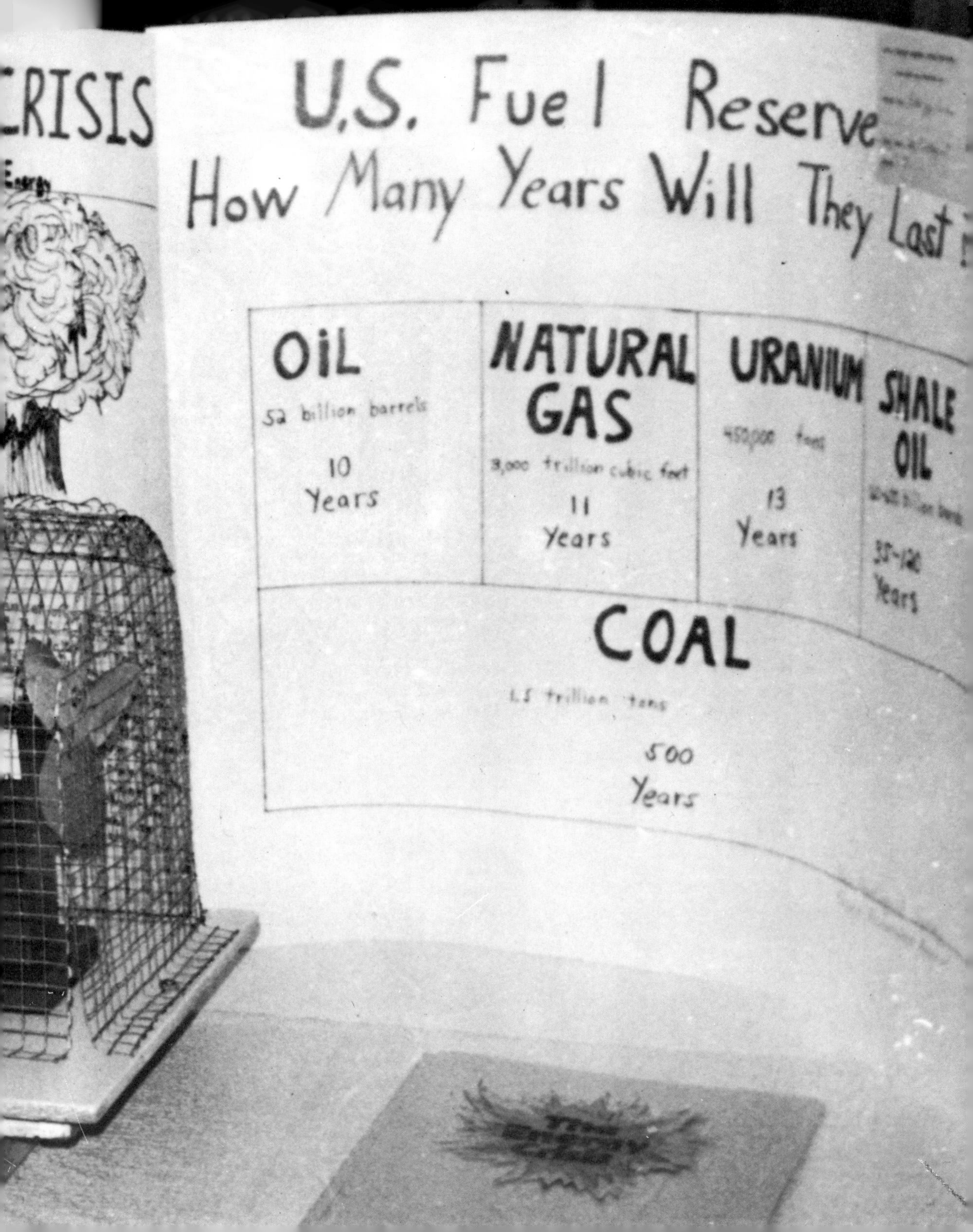
CRISIS
U.S. Fuel Reserve
How Many Years Will They Last
OIL
52 billion barrels
10 Years
NATURAL GAS
11 Years
URANIUM
13 Years
SHALE OIL
Years
COAL
1.5 trillion tons
500 Years

Left: temperature project.
Above: comparative anatomy project.

Books with Project Ideas

☐ **General Projects**

Barr, George. *More Research Ideas for Young Scientists.* New York: McGraw-Hill Book Company, 1961.

————. *Research Adventures for Young Scientists.* New York: McGraw-Hill Book Company, 1964.

Barrett, Raymond E. *Build It Yourself Science Laboratory.* Garden City, N.Y.: Doubleday & Co., Inc., 1963.

Benrey, Ronald. *Ideas for Science Fair Projects.* New York: Arco Publishing Co., Inc., 1962.

Branley, Franklyn M. *Experiments in Sky Watching.* New York: Thomas Y. Crowell Company, 1967.

Brown, Bob. *Science Treasures: Let's Repeat the Great Experiments.* New York: Fleet Press Corporation, 1968.

De Vries, Leonard. *Second Book of Experiments.* New York: Macmillan Company, 1964.

————. *Third Book of Experiments.* New York: Macmillan Company, 1965.

Freeman, Mae B. and Freeman, Ira M. *Fun with Scientific Experiments.* New York: Random House, Inc., 1960.

Milgrom, Harry. *Exploration in Science: A Book of Basic Experiments.* New York: E. P. Dutton & Company, Inc., 1961.

Moore, Shirley, ed. *Science Projects Handbook.* New York: Ballantine Books, Inc., 1960.

Moore, William. *Your Science Fair Project.* New York: G. P. Putnam's Sons, 1964.

Press, H. J. *Science Projects for Young People.* New York: Van Nostrand Reinhold Company, 1970.

Sawyer, Roger Williams and Farmer, Robert A. *New Ideas for Science Fair Projects.* New York: Arco Publishing Co., Inc., 1967.

Schwartz, Julius. *It's Fun to Know Why: Experiments with Things Around Us.* New York: McGraw-Hill Book Company, 1952.

Stone, A. Harris. *Science Project Puzzlers: Starter Ideas for the Curious.* Englewood Cliffs, N.J.: Prentice-Hall, Inc., 1969.

————. *Science Projects that Make Sense.* New York: McCall Books, 1971.

Wyler, Rose. *First Book of Science Experiments.* New York: Franklin Watts, Inc., 1971.

□ **Plants and Animals**

Brainerd, John W. *Nature Study for Conservation: A Handbook for Environmental Education.* New York: Macmillan Company, 1971.

Budlong, Ware and Fleitzer, Mark H. *Experimenting with Seeds and Plants.* New York: G. P. Putnam's Sons, 1970.

Hillcourt, William. *Fun with Nature Hobbies: A Cub Scout Project Book.* New York: G. P. Putnam's Sons, 1970.

————. *Fieldbook of Nature Activities and Conservation.* New York: G. P. Putnam's Sons, 1961.

————. *The New Fieldbook of Nature Activities and Hobbies.* New York: G. P. Putnam's Sons, 1970.

Johnson, Gaylord. *Hunting with the Microscope: A Beginner's Guide to Exploring the Microworld of Plants and Animals.* New York: Sentinel, 1963.

Klein, Richard M. and Klein, Deana T. *Discovering Plants: A Nature and Science Book of Experiments.* Garden City, N.Y.: Natural History Press, 1968.

Leskowitz, Irving and Stone, A. Harris. *Animals Are Like This.* Englewood Cliffs, N.J.: Prentice-Hall, Inc., 1968.

Podendorf, Illa. *True Book of Plant Experiments.* Chicago: Childrens Press, Inc., 1972.

Pringle, Lawrence, ed. *Discovering Nature Indoors: A Nature and Science Guide to Investigations with Small Animals.* Garden City, N.Y.: Natural History Press, 1970.

Silvan, James. *Raising Laboratory Animals: A Handbook for Biological and Behavioral Research.* Garden City, N.Y.: Natural History Press, 1966.

Simon, Seymour. *Animals in Field and Laboratory: Science Projects in Animal Behavior.* New York: McGraw-Hill Book Company, 1968.

————. *Projects with Plants: A Science at Work Book.* New York: Franklin Watts, Inc., 1973.

Stone, A. Harris and Collins, Stephen. *Populations: Experiments in Ecology.* New York: Franklin Watts, Inc., 1973.

Stone, A. Harris and Leskowitz, Irving. *Plants Are Like That.* Englewood Cliffs, N.J.: Prentice-Hall, Inc., 1968.

☐ **Physical Sciences**

Beeler, Nelson and Branley, Franklyn. *Experiments in Electricity.* New York: Thomas Y. Crowell Company, 1959.

————. *Experiments in Chemistry.* New York: Thomas Y. Crowell Company, 1950.

————. *More Experiments in Science.* New York: Thomas Y. Crowell Company, 1950.

Feravolo, Rocco V. *Easy Physics Projects: Air, Water and Heat.* Englewood Cliffs, N.J.: Prentice-Hall, Inc., 1966.

Herbert, Don. *Mr. Wizard's Experiments for Young Scientists.* New York: Doubleday & Company, 1959.

Kadesch, Robert R. *Crazy Cantilever and Other Science Experiments.* New York: Harcourt Brace Jovanovich, Inc., 1965.

Neal, Charles D. *Safe and Simple Projects with Electricity.* Chicago: Childrens Press, Inc., 1965.

Rosenfeld, Sam. *Magic of Electricity.* New York: Lothrop, Lee and Shepard, 1963.

Stone, A. Harris. *The Chemistry of a Lemon.* Englewood Cliffs, N.J.: Prentice-Hall, Inc., 1964.

Stone, A. Harris and Siegel, Bertram M. *Take a Balloon.* Englewood Cliffs, N.J.: Prentice-Hall, Inc., 1967.

Stone, George K. *Science Projects You Can Do.* Englewood Cliffs, N.J.: Prentice-Hall, Inc., 1963.

————. *More Science Projects You Can Do.* Englewood Cliffs, N.J.: Prentice-Hall, Inc., 1970.

Sweezy, Kenneth M. *Chemistry Magic.* New York: McGraw-Hill Book Company, 1956.

Van de Water, Marjorie. *Edison Experiments You Can Do.* New York: Harper and Row, Publishers, 1960.

Acknowledgments

The author is indebted to the following pupils who contributed excerpts from their research projects:

(1) Gary Dekow, Kennedy Junior High School, Woburn, Mass.; Teacher, Louise Mary Nolan

(2) Ted Simondes, Warren School, Wellesley, Mass.; Teacher, Doris Mackey

(3) Mike Buckley, Warren School, Wellesley, Mass.; Teacher, Doris Mackey

(4) Chris Funk, Warren School, Wellesley, Mass.; Teacher, Doris Mackey

(5) Janet Cranshaw, Warren School, Wellesley, Mass.; Teacher, Doris Mackey

(6) Laura Walsh, Warren School, Wellesley, Mass.; Teacher, Doris Mackey

(7) Linda Garmon, Fiske School, Wellesley, Mass.; Teacher, Marcie Lifson

(8) Linda Garmon

(9) Mike Buckley

(10) Kathryn Coules and Karlene Beall, John Glenn Junior
     High School, Bedford, Mass.;
     Teacher, James Rouvalis
(11) Laura Walsh
(12) Karen Scherrer, Fiske School, Wellesley, Mass.;
     Teacher, Marcie Lifson

Index

About the Author

David Webster is a former elementary and junior high school science teacher and served for four years as Director of Science for the Lincoln, Massachusetts school system. He is now a science consultant for the Wellesley public schools, and has written numerous science-activity articles for children's magazines.

Two of Mr. Webster's many books have been published by Franklin Watts — *Photo Fun* and *Track Watching,* the latter of which received an Honorable Mention Award from the New York Academy of Science and was selected as one of the 101 outstanding children's trade books in the field of science for 1972 by the National Science Teacher's Association-Children's Book Council Joint Liaison Committee.

A man of boundless energy and imagination, Mr. Webster works as a carpenter and housebuilder, is a talented photographer, is co-owner and co-director of Camp Netop in Maine, and has been a Boy Scout leader for many years. He and his family live in Lincoln, Massachusetts.